June '16

Out of Breath

Mel ~~McMahon~~

Mel McMahon (signature)

SUMMER PALACE PRESS

First published in 2016 by

Summer Palace Press
Cladnageeragh, Kilbeg, Kilcar, County Donegal, Ireland
and
31 Stranmillis Park, Belfast BT9 5AU

© Mel McMahon, 2016

Winner of the Best Irish Printed Book
and Best Irish Printed Magazine 2015

Printed by Nicholson & Bass Ltd.

A catalogue record for this book is available from the British Library

ISBN 978-0-9954529-0-9

This book is printed on elemental chlorine-free paper

for
Bernadette

Acknowledgements

Some of the poems in this book have previously appeared in: *Poetry Ireland*; *The Honest Ulsterman*; *Fortnight*; *Books Ireland*; *Signals* (edited by Adrian Rice, Abbey Press, Newry) and *A Conversation Piece, Poetry and Art* (edited by Adrian Rice and Angela Reid, Abbey Press, Newry).

My thanks to Mark Roper, Seamus Heaney, Michael Longley, Pat Mooney, Dymphna Taggart, Medbh McGuckian, Michael Quinn, Adrian Rice, Joe Stewart and Dr. Brian Hanratty.

Biographical Note

Mel McMahon was born in Lurgan in 1968. With Adrian Rice, he co-founded the Abbey Press in 1997. His work has appeared widely in journals and anthologies and has been broadcast on BBC Radio Ulster. He has been short-listed for the Beehive International Poetry Prize and was a prize-winner in the FSNI International Poetry Competition (2015). He is currently Head of English at the Abbey Grammar School in Newry, County Down.

CONTENTS

Readings	11
Newcastle Drive	14
Prince Caspian	15
Sunday	16
Remembrance	17
Flight	18
Take This To Your Father	19
Lift	20
Ties	21
From a Forgotten Notebook	22
Opening	23
In Dordogne	24
Last Journey	25
Caller	26
Telephone	27
Snib	28
At My Parents' Graveside	29
Fada	30
As It Was	31
Butterfly	32
Here and Now	33
Summer Roadsides	34
Lovers in Fields	36

The Ornithologists	37
Summer	38
The Musicians	39
Listening to Churchill	40
The Kingfisher	41
The Disappeared	42
The Maze	43
When We Fall	44
The Open Grave	45
Last Night	46
Cloghogue Martyrs	47
Storm	48
Hut	49
State of Play	
The Wait	50
Internment	52
Conkers	53
Find	55
In Play	56
Running the Sheds	57
Quoits	58
Inertia	59
Visiting the Kite Man	60
Tawls	62

Readings
for Maria

1: Sloan Street, 1976
So many days I remember them
neighbouring a blazing fire,
him, folding and unfolding *The Irish News*,
setting his spectacles like a target finder,
wetting his lips on a cup of tea
before giving the paper a shake-rustle
to agitate the death columns into life.

As notices were read
the names and parishes
huddled together,
crossed the solemn columns.
His voice rose and dipped
like contours on a map,
and my grandmother listening.

Sometimes there was a silence,
the tick-tock of a clock,
and then her comment:
I thought he died a while ago.

And his reply:
*He was a long time dead
before his name made it here.*

II: *Taghnevan*
For the new visitor, at first,
there was a smile, a shyness,
an extra flush in her ruddy cheeks,
a desire to have fun, and awkward,
not wanting to be the centre of attention.
But as the room loosened with laughter
the kettle would be boiled
and there would come the request:
If it's tea you're making
could you make it with leaves?

Then there was the lifting of wedding china
from the cabinet, her very best.
And the ritual began.

The cups and teapot were scalded
before a hefty measure
of tea leaves was swept up in hot water
and the plain and everyday
met the world of a far-off orient
to provoke the future into releasing
its store of personal cargoes.

In the theatre of small talk,
comments shrank by the syllable,
as giant sips of tea searched
for the soothsaying sediment
landscaping the bottom of a cup.

But before the reading, another ritual.
For the uninitiated
there was a turning of the cup,
three times clockwise,
a trade-off that seemed to say,
Before we enter the future
we must secure the present
and lock it firmly down
in case we lose hold.

And as she cupped her best china in her hands
I watched the faces of the visitors,
and hers, as she pondered shapes in the silence.
And before those clotted leaves began to speak
I watched her rotate
a willow-patterned world in her hands.

Newcastle Drive
for Gavin

Such an ordeal back then
– getting us all ready,
checking the car,
locking up the house,
strapping ourselves in
and heading off to Newcastle –
our Sunday saunter down the road.

Knowing then that a wrong move
or a wrong word could mean
I'll pull this car over,
we chastened ourselves,
obedient as winter grass,
and sometimes hummed along
to whatever tune he fancied –
hymns he had to sing
at a forthcoming wedding (or funeral)
or Jolson, his favourite.
So we travelled through *April Showers*,
an *Anniversary Waltz*, his pick,
word perfect, note perfect,
and as he finished a song
and satisfaction checked itself
against the silence,
I began to hear the tyres'
tiny thrumming on the tarmac;
could see the tree-lined road up ahead
swaying us around bends to Newcastle
as the day slowly unwrapped itself,
ribbon first.

Prince Caspian
for Anne-Marie Poynor

There were Saturday nights
spent by the fire, watching episodes
of *Starsky and Hutch* or *Match of the Day*,
nights closed by chapters of *Prince Caspian*
before turning off the light,
but not for sleep…

For sleep couldn't come until
I could hear his footsteps
in the alleyway outside,
hear our gate opening, then the back door,
then his footsteps on the stairs,
his clumsy gait on the linoleum floor,
feel his beery breath above my face
as he checked on my sleeping…

And as my heart shrank
like a lost freedom
in the dark cell of my chest,
I eloped on horseback,
became Prince Caspian
on a lean, black steed,
confident enough to take a horse's reins,
to travel, fearless, through dark forests,
my royal cape rushing out behind me,
horizontal with speed.

Sunday
for Brian Hanratty

Once, as I approached the age of twelve,
I was handed the weekly envelope
to be given up at Mass. *Now, don't
be standing near the back. Don't leave
early and don't be home for dinner late!*
I set off with the light package of change
but never made it past the chapel gate.
I missed Mass to miss the gospel's guilt range.

Beneath a bridge I peeled back the gum
and took out the coins to spend on sweets.
I ate them quickly before getting home.
In the scullery, dishes were out, the table set.
I wanted to confess but avoid disgrace.
Self-hate raged as pride smiled from her face.

Remembrance
for Catherine and Nuala

On Sunday evenings, having spent mornings
shelling peas, peeling potatoes
and roasting the Sunday dinner,
she would relax by smoothing clothes.
'Smoothing' rather than ironing.
She sank her arms elbow-deep into the washing basket
and began her haul as she listened to the wireless:
*Rock of Ages, Down by the Riverside,
Johnny I Hardly Knew Ya…*

Flight
for Róisín Kelly

As she lay dying
a dipping breeze
took a bee through
the open window
of her bedroom.
Too far gone to be startled
she watched its clumsy crawl,
its gentle approach
to the floral stitching on her duvet.
And there it rested,
almost still, throbbing
like a glossy jewel,
its wings and legs
an impossible match
for its dutiful weight.

And as she watched
for that moment,
the landscapes loaded in its legs
– open fields clotted
with children and clover,
riverbanks crumbled with buttercups,
meadows shimmerous with life –
spread out like a picnic blanket
in front of her
with her childhood
and its atlases of days.

Take This To Your Father
for Francis McMahon

Take this to your father, she said.

And there I stood, my breath tightening,
holding a cup of hot tea in my hands,
my index finger suddenly spineless,
trying to grip the elaborate inverted C
of the cup handle,
my eyes fixed on the trembling brown surface
as my feet shuffled, like someone in old age –
or Christ, putting trust in His Father,
as He stepped onto the walkable water.

Lift
for Phyllis and Jarlath McGeown

Unable to sleep, I stare into
the dark valley silence
from my bedroom window.
From somewhere comes
the noise of a car horn;
a short, sharp, valedictory sound.
I hear the bar slide open
across the gate in our back yard,
see her return from her evening shift

and my ten-year-old heart lifts.

Ties
for Anne McParland

Such a simple deed
now marks the passage of time.
I bend to tie my mother's shoes
where once she bent for mine.

From a Forgotten Notebook
for Margaret and Jackie McKee

How much he loved her
was not always obvious to me –
the way he darted out of the house,
unnoticed, to place bets,
to be with others, those early years of drinking.

But when she was gone
I could see the turbulence of grief
burnt deep in lustreless eyes;
written in the veins wrestling beneath his flushed skin;
in the stray hairs his razor blade had missed;
in the blisters his blind hands
had taken from stoking reluctant fires.
And also the stale smells that took up residence in his clothes,
his suits suddenly shiny at elbow and cuff,
too big in the shoulders.
No matter how much he distracted himself
with Hollywood's Old Testament of schmaltz,
no song by Lanza or Nelson Eddy
could saccharin the darkness in which he wept.
And his glasses so grimy,
no Eurydice could have been seen,
even if he could have called her back.

Opening
in memory of Elizabeth McMahon: 1935-2004

Ten years after the anniversary of her death
her last moments recycle themselves
in the darkness of a winter bedtime.

Still, on a hospital bed, as if rehearsing her own wake,
cancer circuiting the districts of her organs,
blood broadcasting the news of her imminent demise,

I watched her face for clues of last thoughts,
held her cold, still, talkless hand in mine
and found myself freed from the gibbet of grief

remembering when those hands had passed me pegs,
unhooking clothes from the washing line,
the starched air blooming in our lungs,

above us, the sky full of stars, open.

In Dordogne
for Philip

The morning he died
I was in a Carmelite monastery
in the Dordogne.
The dark sky swacked out rain
like a leather belt doubled up
and pulled back tightly upon itself.
Inside, the stained glass windows
ran in fissures
of long-fingered lightning,
the nuns' choir retaliating
with a sprinkle of hymns
to sweeten the sky's darkness,
cloud grumble.

In the balcony reserved for visitors
we sat and spoke of home,
about my father's love
for songs and space.

In the pocket of my shorts
the screen of my mute phone glowed.
Again. And again. And again. And again.

Last Journey
in memory of Patrick McMahon: 1937-2010

The journey of eels from the Sargasso
to the Bann Foot lured him each summer.
On the last day that I saw him
I took him to look for eels. A man
he hadn't seen in decades
spoke to him about matches,
their former games,
and gave him a bag of eels for free.
I took him home and cooked them.

And that was it.

Goodbyes were said and a door
that had been ajar for forty years
suddenly lost its hinges and disappeared.

Caller
for Ronnie Cunningham

How many hours in the early morning
were broken by a cupboard snapping shut,
the kettle being boiled, a chair pulled out,
his *Twelve Steps* book opened, just in case?

On the morning of his funeral,
a caller, early, his timing almost biblical:
Your dad did a lot that wasn't seen.
His heart was as big as a bus.

Telephone
for Jennifer

I
Large and white with numbers big enough
for an elephant to stand on –
my dad's last telephone.

He would rarely use it, preferring instead
a house call.
When it rang he was often watching horse races
or getting ready to go out.

It is the phone he used
to call me, out of the blue,
one evening in France,
three days before his death,
upbeat about the summer trips
we could go on when I got home.

Holding its dead receiver in my hand,
I imagine my father listening.
My fingers tread the causeway of numbers
to a place that can't be reached.

II
*If your call lasts more than two minutes
it should be a letter*, he would say.

So as teenagers, our calls were quick
to avoid dirty looks, a fight.

Now that I want to speak to him
I can only stare at this telephone,
re-imagine conversations, and write.

Snib
for Pat Mooney

He died when I was away in France.
So I never got to say the words that the others did.

As I quit his house now for good
I wish I could return, leave his front door on the snib.

At My Parents' Graveside
for John and Margaret Dummigan

The love I feel towards them
runs unbroken in currents
to those resting beneath these stones.

No prayers, no tears,
no surge of grief can uncoffin soil
or animate their bones.

Fada
for Adrian Bradley

A pointed line
striking into words
making the hurt vowels longer –
a half-roof, a slope
for the tongue
to descend
into the holes of sound,
the groves of knowledge.
A spade shaft,
the head missing.
My grandfather
looking over his newspaper,
raising an irate eyebrow,
fada-shaped.

As It Was
in memory of Joe Kane

One story told to me,
carried from almost seventy years ago:
two brothers in a seaside town
attend school. A cold school. A dark school.
A school with little room for warmth or light.

One brother plays, holds lumps of plasticine,
and turns them like prisms in his hand.
He makes a tractor,
moulds it to the shape of one
he's seen in a neighbour's field.
He furrows the classroom floor
and *brumms* off his morning tiredness
into daydream. He can smell the tractor engine,
the turned, compliant earth, and hear the birds
as they dither from branch to branch
pick-pocking the air with song.

But he does not hear the Master
speaking to him. Not the first time.
Not the second time. Not the third time.

His brother, now in old age,
wakens some nights having re-watched
the playback of kicks, of roars, of tears,
the curled body shrinking under the weight
of sobs, snivels, silence.

And though the Master is now dead
and the classroom gone,
no words, no hand cupped across a shoulder,
no music from birds or tractors
can sweeten the helpless guilt;
still the stirred sediment of his dreams.

Butterfly
for Mark Roper

I came across it in winter
clutching the sapless concrete
of our garage wall: its legs, air incarnate,
anchored like a satellite's spindly probes
on a moving comet, its wing angle
ridiculously perpendicular.

The freedom of fragile flight forgotten,
no sunlight to sugar its veins,
it had sealed up its wings, crypt-tight,
as if the greyness of these days
didn't deserve such colour,
such life, such surprise.

Here and Now
in memory of Bernard and Margaret Dummigan

When their evening chores were done
– the pigeons seen to, the garden locked off –
a chair would be taken from the kitchen
and placed in the scoured half moon
of their front doorstep. Unaware of the toils
of the day marking her pinafore,
she'd sit, staring, as if doing so
were an advancement in the here and now.
He'd join her at the jamb of the door
and they'd both stare as if being there
could salvage the last moments of the day,
could bale them up like fodder for darker months.
Oh, and the sky, blue, so clear, almost void of its gravity.

And them looking out, knowing, without saying,
You can see so much from here.

Summer Roadsides
for Joe Smyth

Each summer
I notice
which flowers
fill the hedgerows,
before I am struck
by how much
the roads have filled
with dead foxes,
badgers, dogs,
which end up
nothing more
than scraggy pelts
scabbing the tar.

And then
the many birds –
thinned so much
by fast
blind tyres
I can hardly tell
their breed.
Their burst bodies,
their twisted wings
(everything
inside out)
misleads my guess.

Soon, I forget them.

But sometimes here
when I'm informed
of bodies
tied and dumped,
I cannot help but imagine
a dead bird nearby,
its opened body
wounding the tar,
a warm wind
publishing its tiny death,
its broken wing
flapping in late surrender.

Lovers in Fields
for Paul McCann

There were many lovers in fields tonight.
Horses eyed each other from afar

testing the warm air. Meeting, their necks entwined,
bodies fell with easy strength to ground.

I watched cars sneak up to the Lough's shore.
Engines snoozed as couples unbuttoned love

to their drifting getaway music.
Across the water fishermen's lamps

sneezed on and off in claps of light.
And as a patrolling helicopter cast a red lure

on the water, the moon shone down a torch-like eye,
making even the dust spectacular.

The Ornithologists

Reaching the Lough's edge
after this long journey
was an intention I had harboured
for months: you, beautiful, and me

alone in an old bird hut
where a solitary cobweb against the paneless window
caught strange prey –
grebes or swans moving like light

and the spider sleeping.
In generous dark and rain
the water became a horoscope
where I imagined making love to you

as now I feel I did
when I recall what we both saw –
a coot's small head
near the reeds, rising

then falling,
wrecking the noiselessness,
relearning its love
for a different silence.

Summer

Sometimes contentment arrives,
unexpectedly,
and catches you on the hop,
like those evenings, when young,
you'd walk a girl into the woods
– its leaves flickering,
sieving sunlight and shadow –
and as you lowered yourselves onto the ground
you smelt the warm, damp earth,
felt its acceptance on the heel of your hand,
sensed something leave you,
something else
graft itself
onto you.

The Musicians
for Dominic Wadsworth

If peace does last
no doubt brave pens
will charge to imprison it in tomes.

Trapped in local cemeteries,
victims play the music of their loss
through the bullet-holes in their bones.

Listening to Churchill
for Pat O'Neill

Listening to the slow sure march
of syllable after robust syllable
it seemed, for one unearthly second,
as if what would come had been erased –
the weekly, the monthly, the yearly
trips to soldiers' well-groomed graves.

The Kingfisher
for Sabine and Patrice Deyrat

Sad that it took a holiday in France
to get up close to one
lying lifeless on the road
between the woods and the river.
Deceased, somehow decadent,
a drip fallen
from a ceiling
painted in a blush-swirl
of stars and rainbows.

And ornamental – too great
for days of flight and river scavenge.
A flamboyant full stop
on the sterile strip of tarmac,
slipped from the last line
of some long-forgotten pact
between the land and sky.

The Disappeared

There have been mornings when I've woken
before the dawn has declared itself
and I've turned to you
with blood silking my veins
only to be met
by your turned shoulder
or the soft slurred sounds
spilling from your sleep.

So I move onto my back
and the past tumbles over me
like a barely readable darkness
and I lie there, silent,
remembering beds, rooms, houses,
indentations on a mattress,
two spaces where we used to be.

The Maze
for George Henry

The alphabet's one bastard letter
made a difference on the street,
in mouths and on the page.
Today as prisoners get early release
they leave the place that once was home:
Home with an *aitch*, *home* with a *haitch*.

When We Fall

We have taken these bodies
to different places;
to homes, hotels and houses,
foregoing others' shapes and faces.

And then we have flattened out
our days for love or sleep
sieving moments from our tiredness,
seeking bright bullion to keep.

But sometimes when bed sheets
become a tundra
and the distance between us
lies toxic and deep

a hand finding another hand
can numb a gnawing pain,
can silence a bad love song
before its chords refrain, refrain.

The Open Grave

Light dripping in through shifted slates
encouraged scribbles of ivy to plunder
the paint-blistered walls of the old church.

Outside, moss masked names
on the weathered headstones.
The site's mystery receded

when we found an open grave,
its stone tipped back
exposing two shameless skeletons.

The long scent of their silence
rose to sing of the validity of love
so that we, too, rolled back the slab

from all our touches and kisses,
all lovers' rehearsals in fields and cars,
to question Love's unmeant fossil making.

But rather than stand to ponder
whether our soft words could defy such stone,
we renewed the promise

of those sleeping beneath us,
turned to each other and embraced,
held hands, began our long walk home.

Last Night
for Seamus Heaney

The last night I had was spent in church,
in the half-darkness, in total calm.
The softly lit marble altar shone, clean as bleached bone.
The stained glass windows with their stories of saints,
their glossaries of narratives, held me.
The presence of the confessional
promised absolution. The covered baptismal font
suggested a beginning. The worn brass lips
of an offertory box demanded no dues.

I was there on my own, in silence, and lost in words:
words spoken, words thought, vows made –
tangled in the promises made by people,
promises kept in prayers and books.
I could sense the weight of hope on the indented kneelers,
the sour tang of brief escape from the everyday.
Yet I rested easy and felt at home,
the air ghosted by alb and soutane,
incense and thurible, chasuble and crucifix.
And years of hymns caught in the rafters
dropped like drizzle
as I lay there waiting to be cut adrift.

Cloghogue Martyrs
for Jim and Agatha Braham

On Venustae and Auctae,
Speciosae and Verecundae,
Chari, Probi and Rufinae,
there is little to discover.
Whatever ground they walked upon,
whatever words they spoke,
whatever pains their scourged skin felt,
whatever flames their eyes saw,
have all been forgotten.
Today they huddle together
beneath the marble of an altar,
on show, invisible.

Storm
for Pat and Fiona McParland

When the storm arrived in the small hours of night
we were unprepared –
it flicked up slates, whipped off roofs
and found its voice in the dry throat
of our attic.
Our hearts shook
as if our lives had been entered
by an intruder
and our words to each other
were as gentle as the leaves dropping
onto lawns as that wind passed.

Hut
for Padraig McKeever

A secret hollowed in a bush
at the bottom of my grandmother's garden.
On warm afternoons I would dream
in the hammock of its sagging vowel
or shelter from showers in its hutch of heat.

A chamber of tangled branches
preventing the light from slicing in.
It is where I sat to eat foraged berries,
where, seed-like, I came to know
the strokes of rain on the outer skin.

State of Play

The Wait
in memory of Michael Quinn

And there were nights when newly-minted
pre-winter air arrived on our estate
and streetlights, smoked in swirl-skins of frost,
gave the air a spectre-sparkle
and turned street pavements
into the boards of a West End stage.

Our tiny voices burrowed
through the growing darkness
suggesting games:
halio, halio, who's got the ball-i-o?
(never *Queenie-i-o-*
though we thought nothing of it…)
1,2,3 Red Lights
and our favourite, *Chinese Tig.*
The fastest child was chosen
as chaser; sure-footed, frost-able,
a body fulcrummed for flight,
vision and instinct
strong enough to filter deep shadows,
to see those crouching behind
neighbours' walls and cars.

Once touched or caught,
those of us less agile walked
cement-footed and drooped
our arms against the wall.
And there we stood, patiently,
our fingers cold, our noses cold,
our feet growing numb,

knowing that from out of the darkness
someone would be coming;
a brother, a friend or neighbour
to set us free,
to return us to our place,
to the world we had known and left.

Internment
for Teresa and Paschal McCaul

Before the decommissioned mattresses
were taken to the bonfire
they were taken first to be piled high
between two rows of garages on our estate.
One garage sloped up like a runway.

As the bonfire Babelled to new heights
so, too, the mattresses grew.
Children filed like conscripts to climb onto fences,
to scramble for balance at the rear of the garage.
Heart-sick, I limbered up, scanning streets
for relatives or neighbours,
an excuse to climb down,
to take the telling-off and walk away.

Some children, fearless, somersaulted,
turned the dare into performance
but for most it was a giddy step, a wobbly walk
to the garage edge for bearings,
then a return to the rear, a revving of blood
through the veins
and a leap into the unknown,

and also into the lore of those assembled below,
confused to be among neighbours
who would never be named friends,
not knowing what to say next.

Conkers
for Willie McCullogh

I
The adults said that if you put one
in each corner of a room
their presence would annihilate spiders
and restore authority at floor level.

II
In autumn, mornings and afternoons became daydreams
of hurled sticks boomeranging through branches
overhanging Duffy's garden wall. At school
my body tensed at the thought of being there first
in case gravity or a wayward wind
had tugged a shoal of chestnuts to the ground.

Once split, that spiky green opened to a white womb,
a dense talcum pith, white as the inner cheek of a coconut,
smooth as the lining of a new purse – and inside
chestnuts:
        cradled,
                couched
                        nuggets,
their huge navels a powdery dust,
their skins a glow of chocolate grains,
like buffed earth,
shiny as showroom furniture,
whorls of gleam and magic.

Spearing one with a hammer and nail
felt like a crucifixion of sorts.
The soft shell was not meant for such confrontation,
but vinegar, nights by the fire, nail polish
and visits to the dark forces of the hot press
transformed a chestnut into a conker;
seductive enough to lure strings
from rarely used boots and shoes,
hard enough for the open air of battle,
capable of taking hits, of finding rank and number.

And then there was 'taking shots' –
wild swings that whipped the air,
chipped shells or caught knuckles.
And sometimes there was the embrace of strings;
conkers, like exhausted boxers,
hugging each other for balance,
seeking the bell of a final round.
Those 'slingsy' moments helped rethinks,
new tactics, new grips before the final smash.

III
Years later we'd find them,
those conkers, in the darkness of a long-unopened drawer,
amidst the lost currencies of old coins,
dead batteries, the torn strikers of matchboxes,
or a forgotten rabbit's tail.
Far from their sanctuary of branches;
shrivelled, hardened, their gloss gone,
too tired for any fight.

Find
for Claire

Once, beyond the back of my grandparents' garden
in a ground seeded with stowaway huts and holes
we came across a set of library books
missing their return date by decades.

We stood, sun-stilled, the ground kinetic with shadows,
wondering what greatness lay at our feet
to be hidden like Aztec gold
or the rotting corpse of some dark secret.
We sensed the stealth of the absent reader,
their desire for the books to be hidden,
their dream of a return when the time was right.

Some mould had breached the thick empire of pages.
Black spots mottled the landscapes of print
as if grafting themselves onto the words.
But when one book was opened
its dry spine sighed such dessication and neglect
the moment felt sullied, our find unclean.

We returned the books to the ground,
returned our eyes to reading the air.

In Play
for Gerald Morgan

Monbrief Playing Fields circa 1978.
And boys from the new estate
are togged out in new kit
and have called themselves Albion…*Taghnevan Albion*…
despite being far from Albion,
despite not knowing where Albion is.

Slide tackles and slide-rule passes,
crosses, hacks, overhead kicks,
chest-downs, head-downs, runs-up-the-wing,
filling in, holding the line,
nursing the centre circle at corners.
The odd, unknown dog
an unwanted extra, nosing the ball around
with more control than our centre back.

But sometimes, just sometimes,
doubled up, panting, between deep breaths,
face rouged by effort and sun,
there'd come the thought:
Would many days be better than this?

Running the Sheds
for Malachy Conlon

On summer evenings, towards dark,
we moved, feline-footed, along the tops of fences
and stood until all was quiet, until
rooms lost their light and dogs lay still.
Then off we'd go like war planes,
one after one, with a sense of mission,
the older ones leading the way.
Before long we were all running, flying,
all finding a wounded sense of rhythm
as we leapt from shed to shed.
Eyes fixed on the person ahead,
we shunned the growing chasms
that seemed to stretch below,
but kept on running,
each jump a leap of faith,
a leap into the new person
we were making of ourselves.

We ran and ran
until there came a mid-jump draw of breath
seeing kitchen lights come on.
And there, neighbours stood
frozen in surprise,
seeing our springing silhouettes –
no greater than my surprise as my feet
found terra firma
on a height giddy and new.

Quoits
for Brian Dummigan

Handling an old horse shoe,
feeling its curved strength
and weight, standing feet rooted,
caught in two minds, whether
to throw a spinner
or a reverse loop to hug the pin,
the air filled with estimations
on gravity, distance and timing.
All of that went into a single throw
as you waited for the quoit
to turn, to die at the spike;
for faces to change,
for silence to be unspoken.

Inertia
for Michael and Paul McKee

Summer would always bring its crises,
none greater then than finding
recently un-nested fledglings
in their fluffy livery.
Like great chirping buttons
in last year's leaf-litter
they wing-whipped the air
waiting for food, attention.

Needy, experts only on short flights.
We'd sometimes chase them, catch them,
feel the warm, downy throb of them
in our palms and hold them,
all of us feeling trapped, lost,
not knowing what to do next.

Visiting the Kite Man
for Daniel and Sarah

I
I was taken to him after much harping on.
My mother's efforts, created from newspaper and flour paste
were too delicate for wind surges or wind falls
and the heavy crash landings
that tore through flimsy fuselage
on unexpected descents.

In the corner of his sitting room he sat,
style and swagger in his slicked-back fringe.
Everywhere kites straddled kites.
They lay paralysed, immune to the thermals
wafting from his slacked-up summer fire.
I chose one – its skin a patch of the sky's very pelt,
the seams sealing string to posts
neat as any tailor's stitch.

I took it out for some air. It lay dead
on the ground, breathless. And then I ran,
my legs windmilling, the wind stuffing
balls of air down my throat.
And then it lifted, haring after open space,
finding its huge appetite for height.
My skin shone, burned by the speed of its escape.

And what had started as a tug-of-war
with the wind, with gravity, with myself,
slowly eased. The line was out
and I was anchored. I plucked the string
– taut as an electric cable, generous as an umbilical cord –
and from that height looked down with the kite
at my speck on the ground, amazed.

II
That feeling when a kite ascended
and began its toddler-wobble, left to right,
taking the head-staggers
and setting off groundwards, nose first,
before, unexpectedly, righting itself,
finding a steady path,
a sturdy backbone,
to rise, no steering needed,
suddenly effortless,
momentarily free.

III
It was a time when a summer breeze
enchanted kites from sheds and back halls
to lattice the sky
with their giant wish for adventure.
They fluttered like animated co-ordinates,
freakish daytime constellations.

Tawls
for Mark

I
First we found a kerb or wall.
Then a bruiser was volunteered –
a robust, dense sphere of glass,
bulbous, slow, heavy, almost unthumbable.
We ranged ourselves in a line
ready to squat, to hunker,
to throw marbles, marleys, tawls,
all of us judge and jury on the imagined throwing line,
all of us experts on illegal haunching.

Some crouched, panther-like, scrutinising
the plain of tarmac, its pocked crevasses, its razor-blade edges,
its tiny cauldrons of potential misfortune.
Some stood, serene, as if addressing a bowling green.
And then our marbles were thrown –
some in studied, slow loops,
some with a twitch and a flourish,
others with a pendulum-like follow-through.
Decisions on whether to scrimp on pressure possessed us,
as turn after turn was taken,
finger and thumb tense as the open end of a loaded musket.

So much was at stake as school trouser pockets
uncobbled their bulges.
Some marbles were blown upon, some given a lucky rub,
as thumbs and index fingers set their crosshairs
and unleashed their catapult tensions.
Some were cradled in three digits
and squirted like balls from canons.
Others were a comet blur of colour
as briefly the air became a galaxy speckled with toffee,
brandy, rose-tinted glass, dainty parabolas
of hope, expertise and chance.

A dirty tawl, scratched by tarmac, its scars muddied,
carried a swirl like a pleated, glass feather.
Others were frosted, some as clear as summer skies,
some just plain Waterloos,
but some ornate enough for treasure trove.

Marbles on a true line jiggle-bumped
on the frost-nibbled tarmac,
veering past the bruiser's growing force field.
Others seemed to hiccup around its sovereign space
until the tarmac was brailled,
ominous as the shoreline of a D-Day landing.

And still we kept throwing,
until our pockets were bankrupt.

Resignation allowed us to reclaim marbles
not by property but by numbers of marbles cast.

Some loved glass was lost.

II
Now, as memory tilts on the axes of those moments
the heart hops reconfiguring us, our line, the sky, the glass

and hops again remembering the journey of marbles thrown
towards a world into which they, and ourselves, seemed to pass.